Vusirala the Giant

Illustrated by Fred Mouton

Written by Vuyokasi Matross, Sr Cecelia Ntliziywana,
Nodumo Mabece, Phumeze Mtati,
Heather Sheasby, David Whisson.

CAMBRIDGE
UNIVERSITY PRESS

Once upon a time there was a village where everyone lived happily.

One day, the villagers heard a sound like thunder.

The earth shook. Cups and pots rattled in the homes.

All the villagers heard a booming voice. "I want meat! Feed me!"

"Who is singing, Grandfather?" asked a little girl.

"It's the giant, Vusirala!" said the old man. Suddenly Vusirala appeared.

He was as wide as two oxen, and as tall as a tree.

"I want meat! Feed me!" roared Vusirala.

The villagers ran to find meat for Vusirala.

They brought him one cow, two sheep, three pigs, four goats, and five chickens.

The giant grabbed the cow. He crunched it up.

He grabbed the sheep and crunched them up.

He grabbed the pigs and crunched them up.

He grabbed the goats and crunched them up.

He swallowed all five chickens in one big gulp.

Then he stomped away.

"There!" said the old man, "That will keep him happy!"

The little girl whispered, "I don't think so!"

She was right. The next day the giant returned. He had grown even bigger.
Now he was twice as big! He was as wide as *four* oxen and as tall as *two* trees.
"I want more meat! Feed me!" he roared.

The villagers ran to find meat for Vusirala.
This time, they brought him two cows, four sheep,
six pigs, eight goats and ten chickens.

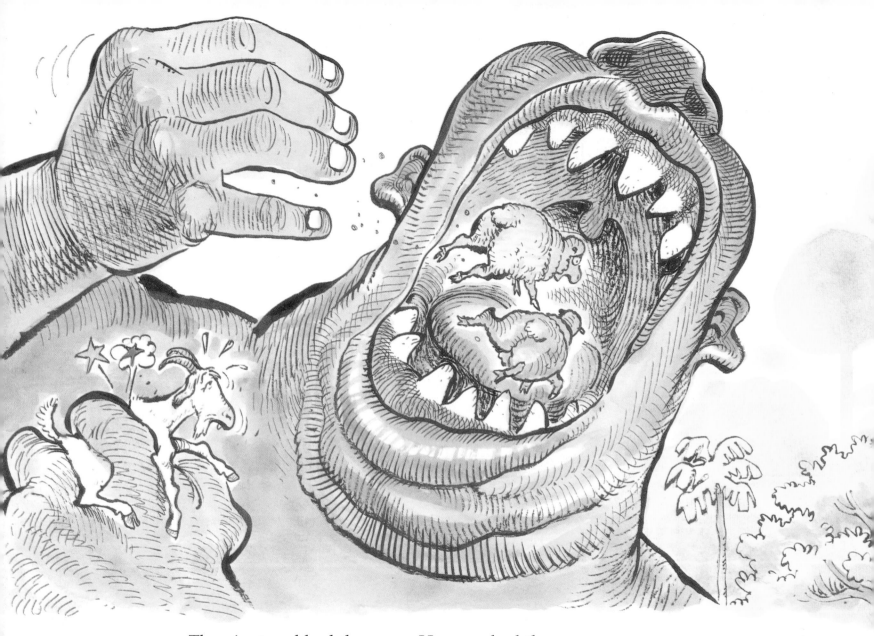

The giant grabbed the cows. He crunched them up.

He grabbed the sheep and crunched them up.

He grabbed the goats and crunched them up.

He grabbed the pigs and crunched them up.

8

He swallowed all the chickens in one big gulp. Then he stomped away.

"There!" said the villagers. "That will keep him happy."

But the little girl said, "I don't think so."

She was right. The next day the giant returned. He had grown even bigger.
Now he was *four* times bigger than he had been when they first saw him!
He was as wide as *eight* oxen and as tall as *four* trees!
"I want more meat! Feed me!" he roared.

Ndifuna inyama,
Ndilambile,
Ndifuna inyama,
Ndilambile.

The villagers trembled with fear. They didn't know what to do.
Soon Vusirala would eat everything!

Then the little girl had an idea.

"I've got something for you to eat," she said to the giant.

"It's bigger than a cow and a sheep
and a goat and a pig and ten chickens.
It's the biggest meal in the world!"

"Where is it?" roared the giant.

"I'll have to take you there," said the little girl.

She led the giant into the forest to a deep river.

She pointed to the water.

"Your food is in there. You will have to catch it yourself."

Vusirala leaned over and looked into the river.

He saw himself in the water.

He had never seen his own reflection.

He was very hungry.

The creature in the water looked big and delicious!

Vusirala roared with greed
and reached forward to grab the creature.
The little girl gave Vusirala a big push!
Paloop! Gdlunk!
Vusirala fell into the water
and the river carried him away.

15

The people of the village were so happy! They sang and danced
and praised the little girl who had saved them from Vusirala the giant.